DON'T BUY YET WITHOUT SEEN THIS SPOTICASH REVIEW

ANURADHA SRIVASTAVA

Copyright © Anuradha Srivastava
All Rights Reserved.

This book has been published with all efforts taken to make the material error-free after the consent of the author. However, the author and the publisher do not assume and hereby disclaim any liability to any party for any loss, damage, or disruption caused by errors or omissions, whether such errors or omissions result from negligence, accident, or any other cause.

While every effort has been made to avoid any mistake or omission, this publication is being sold on the condition and understanding that neither the author nor the publishers or printers would be liable in any manner to any person by reason of any mistake or omission in this publication or for any action taken or omitted to be taken or advice rendered or accepted on the basis of this work. For any defect in printing or binding the publishers will be liable only to replace the defective copy by another copy of this work then available.

Don't Buy Yet Without Seen This Spoticash Review

Stream your favorite music and get paid real cash! That's right, you can get paid to stream on Spoticash. It's the only app that pays you real cash for streaming your favorite songs. You won't believe how easy it is! Just download the app and start listening!

Categories: Marketing Education » Affiliate Marketing

Keywords: Software,Spoticash

SpotiCash *Review – Introduction*

I'm certain you've known about the expression "time is cash" and with regards to music, we can all concur that time is a valuable ware. As I'm certain you're mindful, this explanation rings particularly valid for the individuals who are continually in a hurry - whether driving to work or basically attempting to adjust work/life.

The uplifting news is there is a product now accessible that pays individuals like us for our time burned through paying attention to music! And negative - it's anything but a joke - with the product I am presenting today: Spoticash! This product really pays its audience members in real money for each melody they pay attention to. This implies that you can begin bringing in money without doing anything extra! How about we follow me to investigate this brilliant instrument!

You're presumably similar to the vast majority who figure they can't bring in cash when they pay attention to music. All things considered, you're off-base! Spoticash pays audience members very much like you for their time burned through paying attention to music. It's simple and tomfoolery - you should simply get the application, begin streaming and rake some money!

Thanks to Shawn Josiah, I get the results I wanted

Is *Spoticash* a Scam?

Spoticash is not a scam. However, you may not be able to earn as much as it's advertised on the sales page.

I prefer to be completely honest and transparent about this because I know how frustrating it can be to fall victim to overpromising statements.

While it's within the realm of possibilities to bring in cash with this strategy, don't anticipate being making extraordinary pay. You can procure more than you wind up spending on this, however you presumably will not have the option to stop your normal everyday employment and become a full time music audience with this application.

All things considered, if you need to exploit this fresh out of the plastic new programming, you can utilize my connection underneath and gain admittance to a lot of top notch rewards that, joined with Spoticash, WILL assist you with stopping your 9 - 5 work and become a full time internet based worker.

*Spoticash*FEATURES

- SpotiCash System: 100 percent remarkable, compelling framework. Get compensated $50 Everytime you stream another tune (Worth $297/mo)
- SpotiCash App: The application that makes it all conceivable, Simply login and stream your tunes. That is all there is to it. It requires a couple of moments (Worth $997)
- Preparing Videos: Nothing is abandoned, we made this preparation to take your hands from zero to legend right away (Worth $997)
- Elite Support: Have an inquiry? Simply connect with us and our group will give their all to fix your concern in the blink of an eye (Worth A LOT)
- $241,401.22 Has Been Generated With SpotCash In The Past a half year
- 98% Of Beta-Testers Made Money In The First Day
- 100 percent Never Seen Before Method
- Moment Payments Directly To Your Paypal Account.
- Get Compensated Everyday To Listen To Your

Favorite Artist
- **No Experience required Whatsoever**
- **So Easy, Even A 70 yr old Can Do It**
- **30 Days Money Back Guarantee**

WHAT <u>Spoticash</u> CAN DO FOR YOU

- Get Compensated a normal of $50 for streaming tunes
- The cost builds like clockwork
- Entryways will be shut soon so we can concentrate at aiding our individuals
- No restrictions on the number of tunes you can stream
- Not any more pausing, get compensated in a flash.
- 100 percent protected and lawful
- Just requires a couple of moments each day.
- Works anyplace with any web association.
- At last break out of a futile daily existence and begin benefitting.
- 96% achievement rate with our 309 beta analyzers
- No forthright expenses required at all
- 30-day unconditional promise

Get SpotiCash! What's more, get a demonstrated framework that produce genuine outcomes each and every day. Rather than doing it all alone. You will join many effective individuals. Who had the option to

- Take care of every one of their obligations

- Stop their shocking position
- Have the monetary soundness they needed all the time
- At last have the PC way of life
- Far superior to choice #1, correct? Feel free to get your duplicate of SpotiCash now while you can

SpotiCash Review – What is SpotiCash?

Spoticash is a progressive programming that pays you for paying attention to your preferred music. Get it today and begin bringing in cash while accomplishing something that you appreciate!

The following are five justifications for why this may be a perfect fit for you: Guarantee to procure - You can pay attention to a music - You get compensated in genuine money - There is no base breaking point on how much cash you make every month - It just requires two minutes consistently. Sounds unrealistic? How about you give it a shot for you and perceive that beginning making some additional cash is so natural? I promise you will not be disheartened.

SpotiCash Review – Features and Benefit

- **There are a lot of highlights and incalculable advantages with <u>SpotiCash</u> that I recorded not many** of them as underneath:

- Stream your number one music and get compensated genuine money!
- Make simple money simply by paying attention to your #1 music!
- Considering telecommuting?
- Bring in Cash as a Music Lover!
- World's Simplest System to Make Extra Income
- SpotiCash: Get paid to stream your number one music!
- Get Compensated to Listen to Music with Spoticash!
- It Been This Easy to Make Money Has Never
- "A Miracle System"

SpotiCash Review – How does it work?

There are only literally 3 steps to earn such benefits from:

- Step 1: Login to the software. any of the buttons on this page.
- Step 2: Transcribe any texts and records into audio files
- Step 3: Convert these amazing audios into real cash

SpotiCash Review – My experience in using it?

So you can trust everything from my review

I'm going to give you my honest review of what's inside
this software and how to get real sales with it.

Pros and Cons

<u>Pros:</u>

- Get compensated genuine money just by paying
attention to music!
- You heard right! with Spoticash, you should simply
stand by listening to music and you can begin making a
lot of money! This progressive programming
accomplishes practically everything for you, and you
get all the benefit.
- Constantly acquire $50 each time you stream music!
- Procure as high $395/deal through our profound
channel transformation
- Attempted and tried high changes
- Demonstrated system for your clients to manage an
account with this!
- 100 percent Newbie Friendly Software!
- 100 percent Cloud Based and SSD Servers
- Mechanized Daily Backup
- No Technical Skills or Experience Required
- Inestimable 24*7 help from its specialists
- "Unique Bonuses" in the event that you purchase now.

Who should buy it?

- It is definitely an awesome product for any ecommerce, especially for:
- Any Internet Marketer, no matter what the specialty, who needs to get more cash-flow!
- Anybody who needs to procure from sounds without making their own recordings or being on camera!
- Individuals who need to capitalize on the new "powerhouse sound" pattern however with no gamble or work for them!
- Anybody hoping to stop their 9-5, experience opportunity and clear extraordinary obligation!
- Advertisers who need to totally rule and flourish even in regrettable circumstances like the present!
- Advertisers who need to work for themselves, and get compensated on request at whatever point they need or need to!
- Individuals who need to get everything rolling with sounds/recordings and need the best arrangement!
- Individuals currently effective with sounds that need to reduce down on expenses while additionally further developing outcomes!

Price and Evaluation

Below are the details of different options offered to purchase . Check them out and pick up your favorite one:

FE: SpotiCash ($/$)

SpotiCash gets you paid genuine money only for streaming your #1 music!

Truth be told, you can get compensated to stream on Spoticash. It's the just application that pays you genuine money for streaming your main tunes. You will have a hard time believing how simple it is! Simply download the application and begin tuning in!

OTO 1: Deluxe: Home Income Bundle ($47/$37)

- This update opens and gives admittance to 2 additional programming projects!
- Business License
- Open extra revenue streams to overwhelm and supercharge results up to 10X.
- Get Upgraded To its Ultra Fast SpotiCash Server
- Star Video Training all day, every day Support

OTO 2: DFY ($297/$97)

- Outfit yourself with its DFY formats to get a full SpotiCash business suite
- Complete Setup and General Fine Tune
- Allow us to thoroughly take care of you
- With over 200+ accomplished for you SpotiCash formats suites to browse
- Greatly increment your procuring capacities by opening different gigs with our full suite

- No Technical Skills Required.

OTO 3: SpotiCash Supercharged ($127/$67)

- Open the capacity to take advantage of 3 additional mystery locales to transfer your unique archives to significantly increase your pay!
- Very much like claiming not one, but rather four McDonalds' establishments, individuals will actually want to do a similar measure of work yet compound their profit!

OTO 4: Income Multiplier ($97/$47)

- Easily Make 10x More Money With Your SpotiCash Income Multiplier Edition Without Any Extra Work.
- Implant Our Pre-Selected $1K/Sale Link Into Your SpotiCash Video Magic Link.
- Plug n' Play Our Proven High Ticket Campaign To Your SpotiCash Backend
- DFY Email Swipes.
- DFY Bonuses To Boost Up Sales
- DFY High Converting Sales Funnel
- Computerize, Sit Back and Enjoy the Checks!
- In Depth Video Tutorial

OTO 5: Traffic Booster ($167/$67)

- This overhaul permits clients to ride on its traffic sources and experiences to get additional traffic from the web!

- Tap Into Gold Traffic System Generates $28,900 in 24 Hours
- Drive Unlimited Traffic Directly To Your SpotiCash Pages and Skyrocket Your Daily Sales Without Spending A Dime On Ads.
- It place your pixels to the back finish of its deals pages
- Clients get top notch information for retargeting or profoundly designated purchaser information
- Clients can retarget or make resemble the other the same crowds in light of our done-for-you traffic information and make huge loads of designated high EPCs commissions
- Fitting and play information gave
- Appreciate Unlimited Traffic For Life Without Paying Monthly.

OTO 6: Reseller License ($297/$97)

- Accomplished For You Software Business In A Box (Without Any Hassles, Setup Or Costs)
- Influence Our 7 Figure Team Of Top Notch Designers, Copywriters and Developers (100 percent Access To its Sales Page, Sales Videos, Graphics, Email Swipe, and so forth)
- Remain quiet about 100 percent Profit and Make Up To $864/Sale
- We Handle Customer Support For You
- No Technical Skill Needed

- Video Tutorials Included.

OTO 7: Passive Income Masterclass ($47/$27)

This update furnishes individuals with the abilities to create latent, sans hands pay through our uncommonly chosen different floods of pay masterclass.

OTO 8: Multiple Streams of Income Masterclass ($47/$27)

- This upgrade equips members with the skills to create multiple streams of income through our 7 specially selected multiple streams of income masterclass.

What I Like About Spoticash

- It's Brand New. The techniques instructed inside are exceptionally new to the market and a great many people don't realize they exist yet. By exploiting this offer now, you will be out in front of every other person that chooses to buy Spoticash later on.
- It's Created By an Experienced Internet Marketer. Shawn Josiah has been around for some time now and he knows the stuff to bring in cash on the web and how to help other people do likewise.
- There's a 30 Day Money Back Guarantee. The deal is sold on the WarriorPlus commercial center, and that implies that it naturally accompanies a multi day

discount ensure.

What I Don't Like About <u>Spoticash</u>

It's Too Hyped Up. Procuring $50 on normal for paying attention to music sounds unrealistic. That is on the grounds that, for a great many people, it is. As a beginning stage, all things considered, you won't procure that much.

Not The Best Alternative for People Interested In Earning a Full Time Income From Home. Try not to misunderstand me, the strategies instructed inside can definitely assist you with bringing in some additional cash. Perhaps dependent upon a couple hundred to 1,000 every month. Notwithstanding, almost certainly, you will not figure out how to procure that much except if you set forth some genuine energy into it.

Is There a Better Alternative?

In the event that you're hoping to acquire a full time pay from home, I would recommend investigating all the more long haul open doors that don't include wizardry escape clauses or straightforward frameworks that will bank you a huge load of money for doing close to nothing. In almost 100% of the cases, they don't work that way.

While Spoticash is certainly a genuine application that can assist you with bringing in some cash as an afterthought, it's in no way, shape or form a method for leaving your place of employment and carry on with the PC way of life.

Assuming you're hoping to acquire a few genuine bucks without burning through many dollars to begin, I would recommend investigating the 4 stage framework that I'm utilizing to bank subsidiary commissions of up to $1K per SINGLE deal on top of month to month repeating instalments.

From The Desk of: Arthur Webb

Conclusion

This is the finish of my SpotiCash Review. I trust that my article will loan you a hand in picking the right instrument for your business.

Indeed, I bet that you need to claim this item now. Along these lines, click the deals button now before the cost goes up.

Finally, assuming you like this item, remark underneath and let me know!

Visit to my Official Website:
https://anuradha561986.wordpress.com/

Contents